The Politics of the Watermelon

By Al R Suarez

Table of Contents

Intro

First let me explain what the term watermelon means politically, it is not a racist stereotype. It essentially means, Green on the outside, Red on the inside. Fruit is often used an analogy towards other meanings, such as Banana Republics, to refer to Latin American regimes, of course that is a negative connotation, and usually comes from neighbors from the North like who call them the "backyard". Bananas do not even originate from the Americas, but from Asia, some believe were brought by Europeans, others by Chinese fleets to the Americas prior to the European invasions. I digress. Many people who were Socialist, represented by red or the blood of workers who sacrificed in the struggle, have entered the Green Party, so on the outside they are green. As the Socialist Party USA lost numbers and influence, others who were previously part of that, joined the ranks of the Green Party USA in the 1980s, who finally acquired candidates by the 90s. I have become known through my involvement with the Green Party the past 7 years, shortly after my return to the States from Europe (since 2010), whether in the battleground states of Ohio or Florida, I have supported Greens, but also Socialists, as I have always been a Socialist at heart. With just 7 years I have been called anything from historic Green to veteran Green, the latter causing some confusion as a number of anti war veterans have joined up who served in the armed forces. My point is, that most of the people who have joined GP are new, many of them former Berners, some still holding on to some hope Bernie will leave the Dems.

Nevertheless, I have become an infamous figure in some corners, yes non-grata, but this is part of being an activist, and I continue for the cause for humanity and a better world no matter the controversies. In fact, I would be worried if I had no enemies, especially in groups where I have worked, that means I was not honest or tried to do activism and not just politics. Although we need to work together. It is time for me to go back to my roots, as I see voices of working class, youth and people of color are continually silenced in the "Green locals". This book in no way is encouraging others to leave the Green Party, they may have found more opportunity than me in helping to shape a new society with them. However, we must look at alternatives, movements are not usually led by political parties but by those that are autonomous from the party whether through clubs at campuses, the masses as a whole, etc. I have not literally burned my Green Party voter registration card in Miami, nor have I re-registered as an independent, or anything like that.

However, when I say I have left the Green Party, am talking about the Green local and other groups that limit what revolutionaries can do. Just as the council of "nobels" in Scotland tried to limit what William Wallace did, a freedom fighter for Scottish liberation or independence. Locals can have a role if used right, but unfortunately the upper middle class (bourgeois) white old guards still maintain control and silence others, especially in states like Florida. As for the Scottish example, eventually Robert De Bruce, fulfilled Wallace's legacy, making an independent Scotland, where even part of Ireland joined the nation, and as I mentioned in my first book, I knew a descendant of De Bruce (Bruce Wright). He has had issues with the the state party from his Green local in St Pete as well, and I heard they are not actually recognized by the state party itself unlike other locals. My problems with the Greens here I can escalate but that would be vindictive, rather I want the truth revealed, my truth, to be shown in this book, I don't use the word expose as it has negative connotation.

I have had issues, as mentioned in my previous book, with the Tampa Greens, and unfortunately; after being Interim Alternate Delegate and Outreach Liason for the Miami Greens, the experience has showed me it is time for me to move on. A lot happened in a short amount of time, things were too fast, like a car speeding. The revolution must have rapidity, but also be balanced, nor should it be too gradual like a Fabian. Whether I am considered "active" or not, I consider myself an activist, a water protector, and above all else a revolutionary. Ultimately, these are just labels, words, what really matters is action, my actions speak for themselves, not a defamatory rumor or other destructive force to try to "ban" me from this or that activity, wher at college or in the political realm. We must build, make new ideas, new solutions. Whether resisting for our cause in the fields of Standing Rock, or the jungle of the Everglades, I will continue the struggle. Reformism I detest, as it brings us nowhere in the end, even to a worse condition, which I have touched on at length in previous books.

In the final analysis, this book will focus on the proper role I think Socialists can take to acquire power, and to build the new society we all seek, whether from a resource based economy (Venus Project) or socialist based economy (public health care, education, social programs, etc), or a combination of both, which I will go over in the next chapter. And I am not talking about Bernie-type reform Socialism, but revolutionary Socialism towards true democracy, for the people to have the power, to be informed, and take part in the new society, through unity, organization and leadership, the three fundamental forces. We need a claseless society with workers rights ultimately for equality, not the bourgeois idea that classes be maintained, we need eventually indeed a moneyless and borderless society, a world without empires, that is an inherently Socialist idea to me.

Miami is indeed the frontlines for this economic, environmental front, to take on imperialism, Capitalism, and all its forms, with principles, and in a timely fashion, before the damage is irreversible. This is more important than egos, we must leave our egos behind and adapt, eventually uniting for the common cause of justice for all, the eternal promise, not yet fulfilled. Miami being known as being a city of "gusanos" (derogatory for right wing Cuban exiles) and the like is false, a new generation, of positive radicalism, is upon us. Uniting artists, revolutionaries, and the like, we can accomplish the impossible, history has shown this. The Atlantis revolution is upon us. Am not taking off my green beret and replacing it with my red beret, I wear both, for different occasions, if I could wear both at the same time I would. To revolution symbolism is important, so is civil disobedience. A new platform of the Greens against Capitalism gave me hope, but not enough has been done to implement, in fact measures to reverse that behind the scenes, and not in a democratic or honest fashion, has been done. So it is time to move on. One must know when to insist, and when to desist. The struggle continues.

April 6th, 2017

Miami, Florida

Chapter I

Resource & Socialist Based Economy

I would like to mention in the previous chapter it was dated in April, but in May of 2017 I went over it again and did some editing, as well as changed the title. I will now delve into an ongoing issue with Socialists or even Anarchists who have joined the Green Party, what economy do we seek? What should it be based on? What contradictions would occur? What ideas can we take, and combine, to bring about the ideal, but not the Utopian perfect society which is an impossibility?

Rather than burden myself with coming up with the basic definitions of both economic systems, as I am no expert, but simply an activist who wants to know the best way to implement a fair and just society, I will give quotes with their sources for these definitions; will base my chapter on those quotes and seeing of the possibility of these economies being formed into one, a revolutionary concept. I will start with Jacques Fresco, who is an elderly man who started the Venus Project, I first heard about VP when I was part of Occupy and I have become aware Greens with significant positions in the party, many of whom I have commonalities with, have acquired the notion the ideal is resource based economy, Mr. Fresco himself has said he looked at Socialism and other economic systems and came up with his own one, which is not to say Socialism has not influenced it in some way. The definitions will be followed by an article in its entirety I read after writing the initial draft on this chapter, on similarities and differences between Marxism and the ideas of Venus Project. I will then give a brief comment on the article with its source as well so people can investigate the site from there.

I do not think it is a contradiction that Socialism can work along side it. From what I gather from the definition, Capitalism flies in the face of the society Mr. Fresco and his followers are seeking. Again, those that entered GP with the agenda for RBE (resource based economy) like the Socialist agenda, have commonalities, I will both quote the definition, and the reference to Capitalism. It will also be necessary to define a Capitalist economy for contrast.

"In a Resource Based Economy all goods and services are available to all people without the need for means of exchange such as money, credits, barter or any other means. For this to be achieved all resources must be declared as the common heritage of all Earth's inhabitants. Equipped with the latest scientific and technological marvels mankind could reach extremely high productivity levels and create abundance of resources."

"Individuals and interest groups are governed by laws that demand maximum profit where possible. These laws are inherent in the monetary system prevalent in most countries today-capitalism. The basic principles of capitalism demand exponential growth at all coast causing financial cataclysm such as the 1929s Great Depression in the United States and the recent financial crisis of 2007-08."

(https://www.thevenusproject.com/resource-based-economy/)

Socialist Economy-

A national financial system based on the public or cooperative ownership and administration of primary production capabilities. In a socialist economy, production involves the goal of creating useful services or goods of value. Such economic systems typically employ central planning and use accounting systems based on the labor hours expended in production.

(http://www.businessdictionary.com/definition/socialist-economy.html)

Capitalism is an economic system in which capital goods are owned by private individuals or businesses. The production of goods and services is based on supply and demand in the general market (market economy), rather than through central planning (planned economy    or    command economy). The purest form of capitalism is free market or    laissez-faire capitalism, in which private individuals are completely free to determine where to invest, what to produce or sell, and at which prices to exchange goods and services, without check or controls. Most modern countries practice a mixed capitalist system of some sort that includes    government regulation    of business and industry."
(http://www.investopedia.com/terms/c/capitalism.asp#ixzz4hSLw5hG3    )

"Zeitgeist and 'Marxism'

- Adam Buick    |
- Zeitgeist Movement    |
- Resource-Based Economy    |
- Marxism    |
- Class Society    |
- Peter Joseph    |
-

The Zeitgeist Movement, founded in America in 2008 by Peter Joseph and Jacque Fresco, stands for a worldwide 'resource-based economy, which in many respects resembles what we called 'socialism' (and, if pressed, 'communism'): the Earth's resources would become the common heritage of all humanity and be used in a rational way to provide what people need and to which they would have free access without money; and calculations concerning production would be done solely in units of resources and not duplicated by monetary calculation, as today.

The Movement痴 opponents have also noticed a similarity and have denounced Zeitgeist for propagating 閃arxist Communism◆ still a powerful swear-word in the US. ZM痴 response, in a new guide to their orientation just published on the internet, is to insist that they are not Marxists (see    thezeitgeistmovement.com/orientation). This is true. They aren't. While they are scientific materialists and do see humans as adapting their social arrangements in the light of changing economic and technological conditions, they do not see the agency for these adaptations as some class pursuing its material class interest.

Referencing the        of 1848, they acknowledge that the goal it advocates is a 壮tateless and classless society◆ (Curiously, they omit 僧oneyless◆even though the     speaks specifically of 奏he communist abolition of buying and selling◆) But they go on:

'On the surface, reformations proposed in TZM's promoted solutions might appear to mirror attributes of 'Marxism' if one was to completely ignore the underlying reasoning. The idea of a society 'without classes', 'without universal property', and the complete redefinition of what comprises the 'State' might, on the surface, show confluence by the mere gestures themselves …. However, the actual Train of Thought to support these seemingly similar conclusions is quite different. TZM's advocated benchmark for decision making is not a Moral Philosophy, which, when examined at its root, is essentially what Marxist philosophy was a manifestation of.'

Continuing the same theme, they say 'the Marxist notion of a "classless society" was to overcome the capitalist originating "inhumanity" imposed on the working class or "proletariat".'

They then expound their own approach:

TZM痴 advocated train of thought, on the other hand, sources advantages in human studies. It finds, for example, that     , which is inherent to the capitalist/market model, to actually be a form of     against the vast majority as a result of the evolutionary psychology we humans naturally possess. It generates an unnecessary form of human suffering on many levels which is      and, by implication,    .◆(Their emphasis)

So, unless all they are concerned about is that capitalism is 'technically unsustainable', they too want to overcome the 'indirect violence' and unnecessary suffering that its 'social stratification' imposes on the 'vast majority'. So let's not argue about who is more scientific than thou.

Is 'Marxism' really a 'moral philosophy'? What, in fact, is 'Marxism'? Is it the views of Marx the individual or the system of thought that Engels called 'Scientific Socialism'? It is true that in his earliest writings, just after becoming a socialist at the end of 1843,

Marx's approach was philosophical rather than scientific. He denounced 'political economy' and 'private property' for resulting in the treatment of the 'proletariat' in a way that was contrary to the 'species-nature' of humans. This could indeed be interpreted as basing the case for socialism on a 'moral philosophy' —a view of how humans should be treated but weren't.

However, while Marx never abandoned his indignation at what the working class had to suffer under capitalism, he soon ceased to base the case for socialism on a philosophical theory of human nature. Already in the ⬚ he was criticising other German Socialists for not seeing socialism as the movement and outcome of the struggle of 双ne class with another⬚but as representing 創ot the interest of the proletariat, but the interest of Human Nature, of Man in general, who belongs to no class, has no reality, who exists only in the misty realm of philosophical fantasy.

As Engels was later to put it, in ⬚ based on something he had written in 1875:

'Modern Socialism is, in its essence, the direct product of the recognition, on the one hand, of the class antagonisms, existing in the society of to-day, between proprietors and non-proprietors, between capitalists and wage-workers; on the other hand, of the anarchy existing in production.'

Socialism was a class issue, not a mere moral issue; it was when this was recognised that socialism ceased to be 'utopian' and became 'scientific'.

Engels痴 pamphlet was in effect the founding document (much more than the ⬚ ) of what has come to be called 閃arxism⬚⬚though not by Marx himself. Marx was right about this, as the term suggests that socialist theory was the product of ideas thought up by one man, whereas, in fact, being a reflection of an on-going struggle built-in to capitalist society, it would have developed even if Marx and Engels had never been born and stands independently of whatever they may or may not have said or done. But inadequate as the term is, we are lumbered with it.

So, when, in their criticism of what we will have to call 'Marxism', ZM go on to say the following, they are in fact expressing a view shared by Scientific Socialism:

'TZM is not interested in the poetic, subjective & arbitrary notions of 'a fair society', "guaranteed freedom", "world peace", or "making a better world" simply because it sounds 'right', 'humane' or 'good'.'

They go on:

'Rather, TZM is interested in Scientific Application, as applied to societal sustainability, both physical and cultural. …. The Method of Science is not restricted in its application to the "physical world" and hence the social system, infrastructure, educational relevance and even understanding human behavior itself, all exist within the confines of scientific causality. In turn, there is a natural feedback system built into physical reality which will express itself very clearly in the context of what 'works' and what doesn't over time, guiding our conscious adaptation.'

Apart from the language, Marx had said something similar in 1859 in his well-known outline of the materialist conception of history in his      , in particular:

'Humanity always sets itself only such tasks as it can solve: indeed, on closer examination, it will always be found that the task itself only arises when the material conditions for its solution already exist or are at least in the process of formation.'

In other words, as long as a social and economic system is 'working' there will be no pressure to change it. Marx identified the pressure for change as arising when a contradiction developed between a newly emerging way of organising the production of the wealth of society and a social and political superstructure reflecting an earlier technico-economic basis; the agent for change was a class that organised and benefitted from the new method and which would engage in a struggle with the old ruling class for control of political power. Technico-economic changes made a change of society necessary but the agent of change would be a specific class rather than the members of society in general that Zeitgeist seem to be suggesting

The same applies to the change from capitalism to socialism where, according to Marx, the agent of change will be the majority class of wage and salary workers and their dependents struggling against the entrenched minority capitalist class for control over the means of wealth production.

Insofar as ZM reject the class struggle they can be acquitted of the charge of Marxism� However, as they stand for the Earth resources becoming the common heritage of all, they must be found guilty of standing for

Communism.� (https://www.worldsocialism.org/spgb/socialist-standard/2010s/2013/no-1302-february-2013/zeitgeist-and-%E2%80%98marxism%E2%80%99)


The article makes the differences with Utopian Socialism, similar to Venus Project, and Scientific Socialism clear, again I say, why not both? It is interesting to note that even in the Capitalist enclave of the US, where unlike in Europe moves to get away from a Capitalist system are being made to a more Socialistic system, it is not even purely Capitalist in the US, the fact we have publicly paid police, teachers, firemen, etc, shows there is some level of Socialism. Also all elected officials get public health care, as well as all members of the armed forces, and yet some of them, especially those in Washington, are fighting to not let others, their constituents, have these benefits, and even Obamacare which did not go far enough, Republicans want to reverse aspects of that program.


So now that I have laid out the definitions, do we need see alternatives to any form of Capitalism being in both Socialism and Resource driven economies? The biggest enemies of local business are the corporations, they are a common enemy and have bought off the US government to the extent the government entity itself as become a big corporation. The only thing I differ with on VP that I have found out so far, is that they do not want anyone to work. People can travel the world with no money or borders (I like this idea) but they do not work.

I think if humans do not work even with the travel options eventually they will grow to be depressed. This is the Socialist in me, Socialists do not like laziness, they want everyone to work unless severely disabled, and for their to be programs to help people go back to work if they lose their job. Capitalism is the system where welfare and exploitation is encouraged to benefit the elite, which is inherently anti-democratic. However, this one difference does not mean both systems can work together in the new society.

I have stressed before Anarchism and Socialism can work hand in hand, as they did during the Spanish Civil War against the nationalists and fascists that culminated in the rise of Franco. Ultimately, these are labels, we need the just society now more than ever, and it will take revolutionary change to save us and the world. By the way the term Socialism was thrown around before Karl Marx, but Marx revolutionized the word to mean rapid change. The Marxian concept seems like a Martian or foreign one to many of the working class, that is a failure on Socialists to patiently explain to the masses, as Lenin had. Marx as a man of ideas, a philosopher of intellect, Lenin more of a man of action, a revolutionary, but certainly had intellect of his own while he adapted Marx's ideas to his nation and the times.

Marx's ideas had him go into exile like Lenin, Marx leaving Germany, to France, then Britain, where he continued. Some say Marx growing up Lutheran from a formerly Jewish family has influence on him, but many do not know to get rights as a German and being Jewish you cannot, therefore his family converted out of convenience, the possibility Lutheranism influenced Marx being minimal. However, Marx did not stress the importance of building a political party, which I think in some circumstances is necessary, it was Lenin who picked up the mantle and advocated this. And the time frame between the death of Marx and rise of Lenin was not the big. Anyway, want to stick to the topic at hand. I will go into the importance of work in our next chapter.

Chapter II Importance of Work

What is work? It is only when you are paid? How do Capitalist view work VS Socialists? A Capitalist, or rich person, or advocate of the rich, sees work as the labor of others to benefit themselves. Simply put that is what its basic definition is in a Capitalist system.

Socialists believe work is the duty of society, as a collective, or as a whole, in order to bring in revenue to serve the interests of the society at large. It is almost a Buddhist concept. One with everything. We are all attached to each other and have responsibility to the community, where the word Communist or commune originates from, Communist in particular being a controversial word, in-spite of Cold War hysteria or narrative making it a bad word it is a word that should not scare you.

As a Socialist I not only see work as duty, that is the very basic definition. I see it as a fulfillment of being a human being, to maintain progress and happiness, and feel I have dignity and have worth. It is not something you just do for pay, voluntary work can be more fulfilling, as my mother has pointed out, who is a social scientist in her own right. Should besides what you have given society through your service, you also reap the benefits personally to this and not just have it for health, education or other programs? Yes, I do not think rich people should or can exist, especially the concept of "everyone being rich". For example, if the developing world became developed and we continued to consume as we do in the West, mother-earth would have even more environmental problems on her hands.

Am I saying that the developing world should live in perpetual poverty? No. I am saying we should use less resources, and have a world where everyone can live in dignity, be a little comfortable, but not have to be greedy or shamelessly rich at the expense of others, that is the planet, not just us humans, who are guests on this world. That is how the indigenous people of the Americas generally view the human being, as a guest, not as someone to conquer others, a European concept.

So in the final analysis, work is labor, and the fruits of labor (no pun intended) is what should benefit society, not the individual. Individuals have rights, but so does the society at large. A good analogy is, having a child, the fruit of your loins, does not make you a parent, what makes you a parent is caring for that child until they are an adult, taking responsibility for them, and if you were ever a parent (still have not had that honor) even if the culture says out the door at 18 and they leave, you have the urge to keep them and still seem them as a child. Likewise, you cannot say just because you have worked 5 days a week and earned some money you have been treated fairly, or have given your two cents so to say, to society. Society is one big family, not just immediate family.

# Chapter III Educating Our Children For The New Society

What we teach our children in the homes, effects in great part how they will act when they are adults, and how society will ultimately be. We cannot let our children be naive to the unfairness of this world, and we should let them know they can make the world fair, as optimist-realists. The US has many contradictions, but I am confident there are enough freedoms to try to make the changes we need. My grandfather told my mother once when she said something was unfair, that the world is unfair. That is true but it is not a fact she wants to accept nor do I, I think we can do better. Conservatives have contributed to society as in conserving the environment, which is where the origin of the word comes from.

However, there is now in the Trump era a thin line between conservatism and fascism, we must know history, and the origins of words to truly understand the hidden reality, to wake up like Neo did in the Matrix, to the real world. Many of our words originate from the East, Indo European languages, or from the Greeks, as I have discussed in previous books. The cult of personality, of the individual, is represented in the persona of Trump, and this is a dangerous concept. The recent bombing of Syria made Trump popular again, and defamatory claims that he is a Russian agent ceased, as Trump pissed off those very Russians with this bombing. Is this what makes America great? Perhaps imperial America, but a nation can be great, but not good. I would think one must strive to be of service and good before considering being successful or great, someone of value as Einstein said. Value is not just in reference to profits, just as work is not just in reference to doing something for pay. A person who is valuable who has values, is a productive person to society, who through the fruits of their labor make themselves a person of worth.

We must teach our children to bully is wrong, to stick up for those bullied. This will help them get a good sense of justice, not just an innate one, one based on intellect, like those with Aspeger's, a condition I was diagnosed with as a child, tend to learn intellectually instead of innately. Also, to prevent domestic violence, especially if they are a heterosexual child, they should be severely disciplined and scolded if they ever lay a finger on the opposite sex, even if provoked, like from a sister. They should always respect their siblings, nor should they hit their brother. These lessons can have a lasting impact on how they will be as adults. Practice what you preach. Obviously, the possibility of the child abusing alcohol or beating their wife, would be determined how they witness their parent behave growing up, but it is not inevitable, genetics raises a possibility but not inevitability. Do not make yourself a victim. Try to rise above.

# Chapter V

## What Is Activism?

We must understand what activism truly is, and its role in our cause, in forming movements for social change, justice, protecting water, etc. Activism is a process, one of transformation, transformation is a combo of two words, trans, which means to go beyond, and formation, which means to create. When a person is changed or transformed from one part of their life to another, it is like a crossroads. They have decided from their free will, and circumstances, for one reason or another, to make a change in their mentality. Sometimes maintaining influences of the past, but taking a different, often revolutionary course of action from that transformation, going beyond what they have done, and creating a new reality.

A reality or dream not just based on perception. But one based on the will to change the perception of the people, to new ideas, often to benefit the world, ideas that are not dominant or accepted, but that become more acceptable later on. Such as gay marriage, much resistance from Washington came, even from Dems, but this eventually changed from the will of the people, the change of conscience, commonly referred to as Zeitgeist, which literally means change of conscience in German.

Many who are part of the Zeitgeist movement today were also for VP. The reasons behind the split, as they were once one in the same, I find irrelevant, it would be like talking about the Menshevik-Bolshevik split, there is no point in going off on such a tangent. I would only say the Venus Project-Zeitgeist split happening a few months before Occupy is an interesting timing. Occupy brought together many factions however, at least at its beginning stage. Am not familiar enough with Zeitgeist to go into it as I have with VP, which is not to say I prefer VP. Again, I am a Socialist, but not sectarian, am open to common ideas we can use towards the new society.

So activism is simply being active in the cause you are participating in. Realize part of the word participating is part, you are part of something, taking part, but you are not that something, you should not let your ego get in the way. The role of the activist for social change should be to be one part of something greater than yourself, a drop in a ocean, but a drop that will bring a ripple, and eventually, a current, with that unity, that will bring the tsunami of revolution, the ultimate storm or hurricane, to be like a rolling rock, and take away the obstacles, to replace the old with the new, and the new is that new system you want, for the masses to enjoy, as the current system just cannot work anymore, therefore cannot be fixed, going beyond reform.

Marx, circa 1875

Fresco, present-day

# Conclusion

The idea that "this way or no other way" is quite regressive. I say take the ideas from different philosophies and see how they work together, but with principles. Often for the sake of unity we forget our principles. I am all for unity, but with those who are worth uniting with. What is the use of being in a room where I am not wanted and where people are letting their egos get in the way? I have been in the political struggle 16 years, I am too old, and have been in this too long, to let the drama queens get in the way of my progress. They are obstacles to be avoided, at times confronted, nothing else.

Reconciling with negative forces who have betrayed me, only invites more betrayal. To conclude this book, on the ideas of a watermelon, one who fights for the environment, but also wants to sacrifice for Socialism, and a economy based on our resources justly, rather than greed, I want us to consider unity tactics with principles, towards the common society we seek, for a better world for our children. They deserve better, for the mistakes of the past not to be repeated, for lessons to truly be learned.

The watermelon is a fruit that can only be grown with a seed and the right climate and treatment, likewise the society we seek, must have the right conditions to flourish, and that is what we should work on now in these turbulent times, act as we would in the society we seek, no matter who is currently in the White House, in the tradition of Gandhi and all the greats before who us championed the cause, we must get to the root of problems, and finally solve them, not just protest them. The contrast, the disparity, the contradiction, yes expose all these things, be honest about it all, but offer alternatives, be hope, not just offer hope, as true leaders, not false prophets, be not for profits, but for the good of the people.

I will now leave you with three articles that touch on the Ecosocialist aspect of being a watermelon, first from the Green Party in New Zealand, although not all of GP in other countries is progressive, even the word progressive causes confusion, it is meant generally to be of the Left, although the Anarchists who wants government to end overnight tend to be the extreme Left. Unfortunately, the first article only shows an image and the very beginning, the other-articles cannot be shown in full either-since there is a problem in copying. By the way Peter Camejo of the old guard of the Greens was actually a self-described Watermelon, so not all the old guard were bourgeois or to the right. The second article will be about him, the last will talk of Jill Stein's role with Ecosocialism. Forgive over the course of copying articles into this book some of the lettering turned out Chinese.

(https://fightback.org.nz/2013/05/21/green-is-red-the-case-for-eco-marxist-politics/)

GREEN IS RED: The case for eco-Marxist     politics

MAY 21, 2013     BY     ADMIN

.
(https://mobile.solidarity-us.org/site/node/2088)
**Peter Camejo: A Red-Green Life**

**— Claudette Begin**

THE PROGRESSIVE MOVEMENTS lost a major advocate last September 13th when Peter Camejo died after a long battle with lymphoma at the age of 67. The broad, historical impact he had was obvious in the national media response and the hundreds of emails and blog entries following his death.

At Peter's memorial on November 23rd in Berkeley, California, the range of speakers attested to his persistent dedication to helping the poor and working class from his teenage years to his death. They spoke one after another of his personal warmth, enthusiasm, boundless energy and stream of ideas, strategic thinking, oratorical talents, optimism, and of how inspiring he was to them.

Peter became a socialist and a leader in the Socialist Workers Party during the wave of radicalization of the late 1950s and '60s. Although he played many roles as an SWP leader through the '70s, he was widely known in the party as an incredibly fun and motivational speaker. He was also a mass leader, often intervening strategically in the antiwar movement.

Expelled by the University of California, Berkeley for his leadership of the antiwar movement there in the late '60s (technically for using a microphone without a permit), he was named "one of the 10 most dangerous men" by Governor Ronald Reagan. Despite his differences with the SWP leadership's increasingly sectarian and undemocratic policies, his popularity in the ranks forced them to select him as the SWP presidential candidate in 1976 (during which he even appeared on "The Today Show"), but those differences eventually got him expelled.

Having been a movement staffer for decades, Peter had to find another way to live. Eventually he found his way towards marrying his mathematical talents with his zeal to change the world through socially responsible investing. Progressive Asset Management, a company he founded with other progressive stockbrokers, became an avenue for promoting a number of innovative projects for fair trade, housing for the poor, and solar energy.

He sponsored tours of international activists from New Zealand and Brazil; facilitated the formation of a nonprofit foundation supporting activists in East Timor; and he sought to engage activists in following the transformative movements in Venezuela.

Peter was constantly looking for new opportunities to effect meaningful, mass change. He founded North Star Network in the '80s to bring together serious activists, including former SWPers, with some leaders from the Salvadoran movement. He formed the Progressive Alliance of Alameda County in the hopes of encouraging progressive activists from Peace and Freedom, the Green Party and even the Democratic Party to work together and eventually form a viable alternative to the two-party system.

That experience, and the Draft Nader for President movement within the Greens in 2000, convinced him that the Green Party was such an avenue. The Green Party platform was very progressive and inclusive. He became very involved, familiarizing himself with the structure and methods of the Green Party. He was frustrated with the paralyzing aspect of their consensus process but saw the opportunity for effective campaigns within the Greens.

His subsequent candidacy for governor in the recall election made him a household name in California as he appeared in the televised debates with Arnold Schwarzenegger and the other candidates. Camejo received the highest third-party vote in California since 1934. He captured significant percentages in a dozen counties across Nothern California, even beating the Republican candidate in San Francisco County, and facilitating the subsequent candidacies and election of several Green Party members to local offices.

Ralph Nader, impressed, asked him to be his running mate in 2004. Despite the overwhelming vote they received in the Green Party primary in California and the support they had in other states, the national Green Party endorsed another ticket and they had to run as independents.

This signaled a serious rift within the Green Party with a current that wanted to avoid confrontations with important Democrats. Peter fought against this current, whose supporters increasingly bowed to Democratic Party influence. This eventually led him to lose faith in the Green Party.

His last speech was at the 2008 Peace and Freedom Party convention, where he urged them to choose Nader and Matt Gonzalez as their presidential ticket, which they did.

Peter was a major contributor to the Green Party's base among Latinos, Blacks and other people of color, as well as in the general electorate. He ran not as an individual, but as part of slates which he crafted to draw in leaders from those movements.

He campaigned for giving driving licenses to undocumented immigrants. He helped build the May 1 national demonstrations. He was a constant on Hispanic radio. He spoke out against secret arrests and marginalization of Muslims following 9/11.

Building Progressive Politics

Peter was always happy to support and mentor new leaders as they emerged, befriending Jason West, the Green Party mayor in upstate New York who performed gay marriages. His eye was always on mass proselytizing; he rejected terms from the socialist movement that would unnecessarily alienate people.

For example, he explained the reversing of progressive taxation in California by using one simple chart that documented the significant trend of taxation away from major corporations and the wealthy to the working class. His political contributions have to be seen in the light of someone who constantly sought ways to have an impact, whatever the difficult times politically.

Ralph Nader captured the essence of Peter. On the day Peter died, Nader said "Peter was a friend, colleague and politically courageous champion of the downtrodden and mistreated of the entire Western Hemisphere. Everyone who met Peter, talked to Peter, worked with Peter, or argued with Peter, will miss the passing of a great American."

In his obituary in Time magazine he expanded on this, saying "Peter Miguel Camejo . . . was an irrepressible force of nature. When he spoke out for justice throughout the Americas, not only his body shook, but so did the entire room."

## A new ecosocialist movement?

**Michael Whitehead**, a solar energy engineer and activist based in Pennsylvania and North Carolina, reports on the recent ecosocialist conference in Los Angeles.

THE U.S. Occupy movement has waned from view, but there is increasing evidence of a new wave of American activism and energy building in response to the accelerating climate emergency--under the slogan "System Change, Not Climate Change."

Evolving from this year's historic February 11, 350.org-led protest in Washington, D.C., the latest manifestation of these activities was the Ecosocialist Conference 2013 in Los Angeles, held on September 21, followed by a sister conference in Vancouver on September 23--both emerged in the wake of the highly successful April conference in New York City.

In the face of the climate crisis, a coalition is developing between a traditionally fractious American Left, the Green Party USA and other left groups in a Green-Red "ecological solidarity" that bears watching in the coming months.

- - - - - - - - - - - - - - - -

THE SEPTEMBER 21 event in Los Angeles was held, quite appropriately, in a repurposed (one could say recycled) former courthouse and police station, now a library and African American history museum. In fact, I thought I had awakened in an alternate reality, seeing former police station walls now celebrated with the likes of Malcolm X and other liberation figures (not to mention showcases of not-so-liberating Obama campaign memorabilia).

This was surrounded with a crew of hundreds of socialists of differing stripes, Green Party members, Occupy LA-ers, unionists, aging and teenage ecosocialists, and even more than a few former Democrats, all in numbers and with an energy and earnestness that one veteran activist with personal experience going back to the 1960s told me he had not seen in LA in years.

In the old courtrooms-turned-political workshops, instead of 1960's-era petty misdemeanor and traffic trials, conference attendees weighed topics of the utmost seriousness: How can we save humanity from the seemingly inexorable suicide train of looming climate catastrophe?

David Klein, director of Climate Science Studies at California State-Northridge, led the first plenary, with a sobering summary of the latest scientific climate model findings and a conclusion that cogently and glaringly expressed an opinion shared by most attendees about the futility of traditional reformist "green" activism in solving the global emergency:

> Global climate models predict a worldwide range of average temperature increase of between 2 and 6 or more degrees Celsius by the end of the century. The upper end is potentially a mass extinction event.

> Keeping temperature increase to no more than 2 degrees Celsius is a generally agreed-upon goal worldwide. It has been estimated that carbon dioxide emissions between now and the end of the century need to remain below approximately 600 billion tons to achieve this goal. However, there is a carbon dioxide equivalent of 2.8 trillion tons in known reserves of carbon in the form of petroleum, natural gas and coal underground, valued at roughly $27 trillion to Wall Street firms, and this is included in stock values.

> To meet the 2 degree Celsius goal, the vast majority of the carbon reserves must remain underground, unburned, meaning that Wall Street would have to lose approximately $20 trillion to protect the planet from a devastating future.

> Humanity is thus faced with the ultimate Darwinian IQ test. It is a multiple-choice question. Choose: A) capitalism or B) the planet. We can only have one or the other, not both.

Lisa Lubow, a historian, activist and professor at Glendale College, made a similar point in her presentation, stating:

> Radical changes are needed to save humanity and the planet: to leave fossil fuels in the ground; initiate an emergency program to convert fossil fuel systems to renewables; and radically reorganize our production systems overall for sustainability. The system itself is in direct conflict with the solution to the emergency. The capitalist imperative for unlimited growth through market-driven resource extraction, production and consumption is leading us on a suicide mission. But the system is unwilling and unable to "power down."

In his talk, author and Pace University professor Chris Williams observed that:

> It is increasingly clear to a growing number of people that the ecological crisis is a direct outgrowth of the operation of our economic system; namely, capitalism. The crisis has many facets: environmental racism, energy production, pollution, gender oppression, biodiversity loss, agribusiness and climate change to name only a few. But they can all be traced back to a singular cause: the relentless pursuit of profit and the accumulation of capital.

- - - - - - - - - - - - - - - -

CLEARLY, ECOLOGY and economy are intertwined and inseparable, "two dimensions of one reality" in the words of writer, Green and socialist Scott Tucker in his presentation. In fact, as Tucker observed, the prefix "eco" common to both words, derives from the same Greek root: *oikos*, meaning "home" or "household."

"Ecology" therefore implies the greater household of nature. The word economics contains in addition the Greek root word *nomos*, meaning "law" or "custom". Using the root word meanings, one might therefore say that economics encompasses the customs and processes we use to regulate and operate our home (the Earth).

Ben Manski, Green Party Presidential candidate Jill Stein's 2012 campaign manager and president of the Liberty Tree Foundation, eloquently took this idea further in his discussion, arguing, "The exploitation of human nature and the exploitation of nature are part of the same process. An injury to one is an injury to all--that injuries to oppressed people are borne by the Earth, and injuries to our Earth are suffered first by oppressed people."

Continuing on the interconnection of economics and ecology, Manski argued, "Both practically and theoretically, in the long run there are no boundaries between jobs and environment. There are also no boundaries between class struggle and ecological resistance, and no boundaries between red and green."

The ecosocialism concept clearly has its roots in the Marxian tradition that calls for a re-organization of society to unleash all human potential. As Manski pointed out:

> 'Ecological solidarity' requires a struggle for democracy--what Marx called the 'species being,' the natural essence, of humanity--so that working people can finally 'become the human race,' and self-organize to make the most of our species' capacity to do good, to do right by the Earth, and to respect the rights of nature, so that we may all live in the prosperity that this living planet gives us."

Green Party presidential candidate and physician Jill Stein, in her rousing closing plenary, proposed a concrete program of "next steps" for the System Change Not Climate Change ecosocialist coalition, outlining a proposal for an "emergency green economic transformation," based, in her words, on "on the notion that the accelerating climate collapse intensifies all our struggles--for economic, racial and environmental justice, human rights, civil liberties, peace and democracy."

"While the climate crisis makes all of these struggles more difficult, it also provides unprecedented urgency and momentum for collaboration," she stated.

She called for an "Emergency Green Economic Transformation" program--a "Green New Deal" for full employment, 100 percent clean renewable energy by 2030, demilitarization, and an economic bill of rights (including Medicare for all, free pre K-through-college education as a human right, labor and immigrant rights, affordable housing, and abolishing student debt).